On a warm and sunny October day, the clanging sound of an old school bell rang out across a small farm on Monkey Island, Oklahoma.

The farm wasn't really on an island, and there were no monkeys there, but that's a story for another time.

"Come and get it!" Granny yelled to her great grandchildren, "I've got **blackberry cobbler** and **snow ice cream**! And I have something to show you."

Granny gazed over the countryside and took it all in with a deep breath.

"Happy birthday Ruth."

"We are still here," she said quietly.

"Yes indeed. We are still here."

RUTH

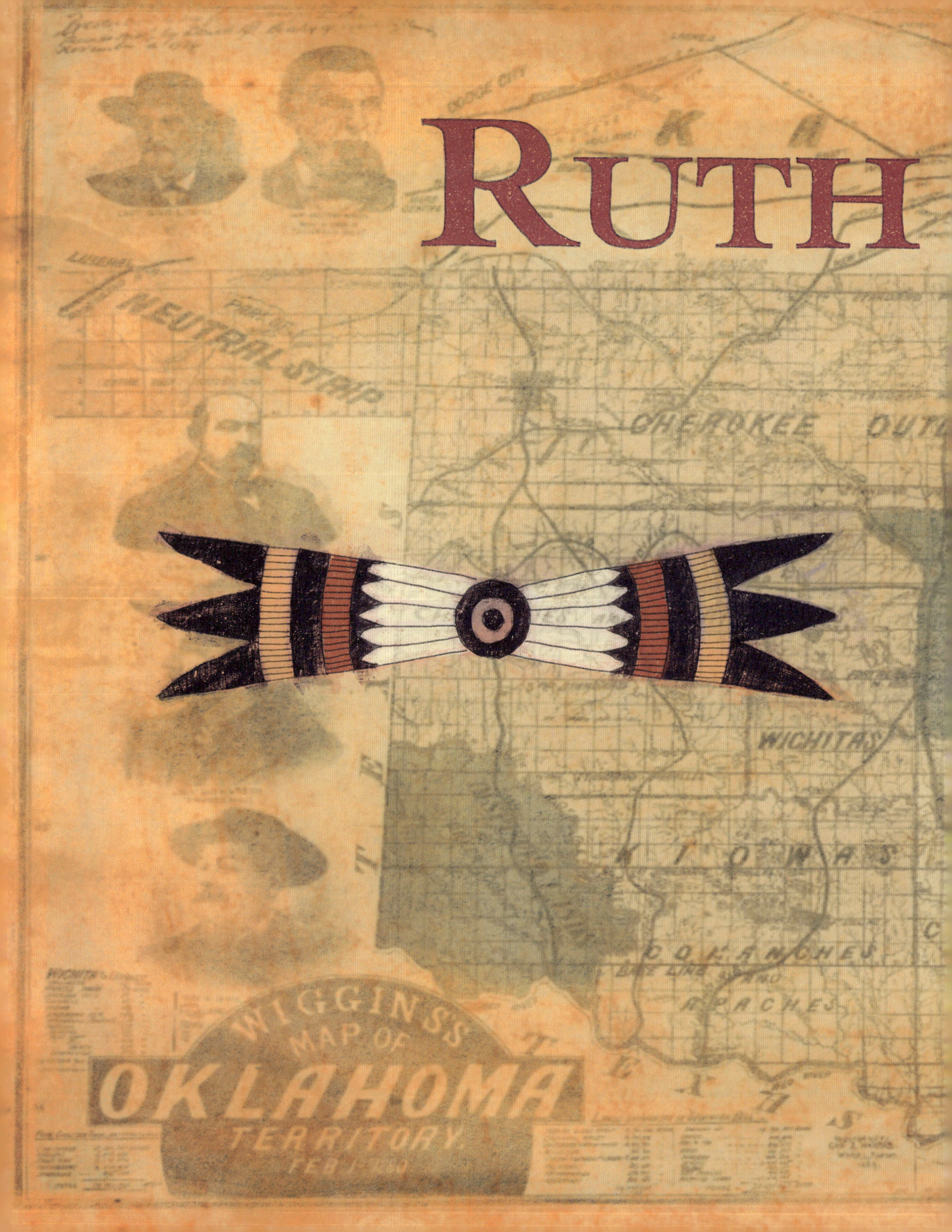
NEUTRAL STRIP
CHEROKEE
WICHITAS
KIOWAS
APACHES
WIGGINS'S
MAP OF
OKLAHOMA
TERRITORY.

Muskrat and the So-Called Indian Problem

The Fight for Native American Civil Rights

Written by JEN LOREN

Illustrated by REBECCA LEE KUNZ

LEVINE QUERIDO

MONTCLAIR • AMSTERDAM

Ruth Muskrat Bronson was born on October 3, 1897, on Cowskin Prairie, in **Indian Territory**.

That's what **Oklahoma** was called before it was a state.

Ruth had six brothers and sisters, all of them lively and smart. Growing up on a farm, the kids had a lot of chores, but they always found time to read books and have fun.

Ruth loved playing in the nearby creek and would often get her chores done early just so she could dip her toes in the clear, cold water and spend some time daydreaming.

THE MUSKRAT FAMILY WAS CHEROKEE

AND MOST OF THEIR NEIGHBORS WERE TOO.

Cherokee families spent a lot of time visiting each other's homes, sharing stories and meals, and talking about what was happening within their tribe and the world around them. Ruth felt she absolutely must know the latest news and would often stay to listen to the adults while the other children ran off to play.

Back then, Cherokee people worked together and helped one another as part of a community — sharing fellowship, food, and supplies.

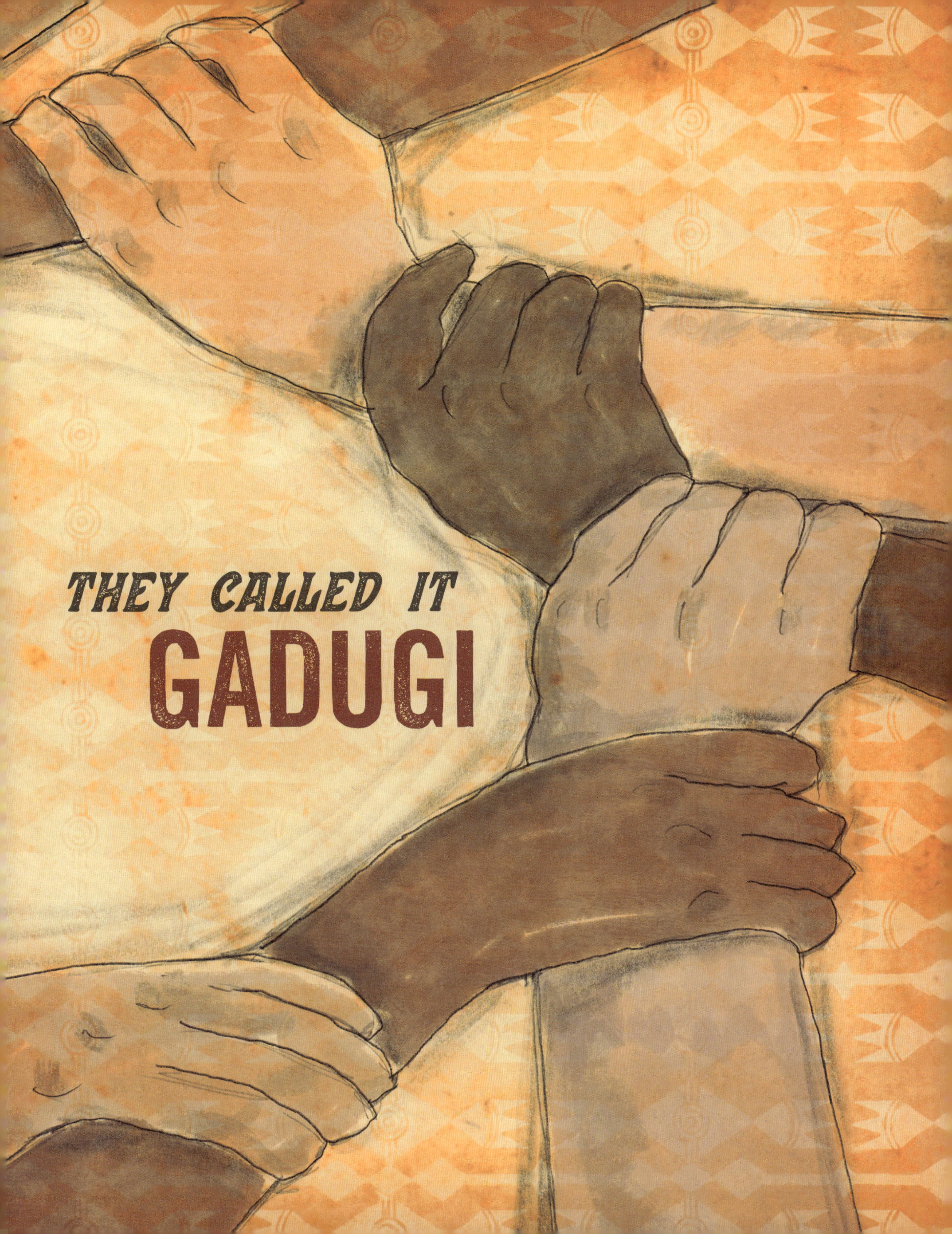
THEY CALLED IT
GADUGI

Inside Granny's farmhouse, it was warm and cozy. "Gather round," she said as the children finished their desserts. "I want to tell you about my sister, who was a very important person." She held up a big calendar with the title *Women Who Dare*.

March, April, May . . . "There she is. Your Aunt Ruth!"

"That's our aunt?!" one of the cousins asked in disbelief.

"Yes, it is," replied Granny proudly. "And she helped change the world."

Ruth's mother, Ida, was Irish and a bit stern. She kept a tidy home and made sure everyone in the family was on time and well-kept.

Ruth admired her mother and often imitated her when speaking to her younger siblings and neighbors.

Ruth's father, James, was Cherokee.

Papa, as they called him, was soft-spoken yet a great communicator, always telling stories and explaining things in a way that each of his children could understand. He had a warm smile, and liked to tell jokes and make other people smile.

Papa loved his Cherokee community and taught the children to have **integrity** and to care for their friends and neighbors.

Ruth adored her father and strove to make him proud.

But as Ruth grew older, she noticed her father had begun frowning more than he smiled.

She would often quiz him, trying to understand. Papa was a leader in the Cherokee community and a member of the **Keetoowah Society**, which kept up Cherokee traditions. He believed Ruth could be a leader one day too, and so, he told her everything, choosing not to hold back details because she was a child.

"The US government wants all Native American tribes to go away," Papa said matter-of-factly. "They're calling us the '**Indian problem**' and are looking for ways to force families like ours to **assimilate**."

"They want us to stop being Cherokee and to start acting like everyone else?"

"That's right," he said. "And they want our land. It's becoming harder for us to fight."

"We must outsmart them," Ruth thought, fiercely.

"WE MUST FIGURE OUT A WAY TO BE CHEROKEE FOREVER."

RESIDENCE:
DISTRICT.
POST OFFICE:
Cherokee
Dawes' Roll No.
NAME.
Relation-ship to Person first
AGE.
SEX.
BLOOD.
TRIBAL ENROLLMENT.
Year.
District.
502
2277
503
National Congress of American Indians
WASHINGTON BULLETIN
BRONSON—MUSKRAT.
THE DAILY OKLAHOMAN
EXTRA!
PROCLAIMS STATEHOOD
6—1044

Granny turned to a giant, mysterious-looking old trunk.

"This trunk has been in our family going all the way back to the 1800s." Granny said. "It's where our **ancestors** kept all their most treasured keepsakes. It was passed down to me and I've added my own treasures."

As the cousins peered inside the beautiful vessel, they thought, maybe it held some important explanations, some answers to life's little wonders?

Ruth's mother encouraged her to learn as much as she could about the world beyond the Cherokee Nation. She began reading the *Kansas City Star* newspaper and collected books each time they visited a neighbor or went into town.

The books taught her about history and how people became the leaders who shaped the world.

Ruth was inspired!

"By getting a good education," she thought, "I can become a person who shapes the world around us and I can help the Cherokee people." She began imagining a United States that respected Native Americans and their leadership and accepted their differences.

A glimmer of hope returned to Ruth's father's eyes.

In school, Ruth became so serious about her lessons that her teacher often called on her to teach the class.

Ruth loved being in charge and challenging "her" students.

For fun,
Ruth would
sit by the creek
and read books about
all kinds of subjects:
biographies, history, nature.
She loved poetry in particular
because it seemed so clever.

Books about faraway places made her daydream of having her own adventures around the world.

"Why not me?" she asked herself and began to think of ways to make that happen.

Some of the boys were starting to get restless. "Now, if you'd rather go outside and play, go ahead," said Granny kindly. "I can stay here and tell stories all day, but I don't expect you to stay and listen."

So they ran outside to go fishing in the lake, but a few of the older girls stayed, huddled around the trunk.

"Go on," the middle cousin, Shannon, said to Granny while Jenny dug through the trunk, not flinching as the screen door banged shut.

What was that buried in the very bottom of the trunk…

They scooted closer.

Life wasn't always serious on the Muskrat farm. At times, it could be an adventure.

One quiet summer night, after a long, hot day, Ruth and her siblings felt restless. Her eldest brother "Toad" dared one of them to sneak out into the night and ring the bell on top of the schoolhouse.

"Ruth will do it!" he called, knowing she was the bravest of them all.

Ruth accepted the challenge and tiptoed out into the dark night.

Ruth's brothers and sisters watched her jog silently down their dirt road and out of sight.

They held their breath.

Just a few minutes later . . .

DONG!!!

The peaceful silence of the night was shattered by the walloping sound of the school bell.

She had done it!

Ruth dared to ring the school bell in the middle of the night, waking every person within a one-mile radius.

Ꭰ a Ꭱ e Ꭲ i

Ꭶ ga Ꭷ ka Ꭸ ge Ꭹ gi

Ꭽ ha Ꭾ he Ꭿ hi

Ꮃ la

As Granny pulled the keepsakes, one-by-one, from the trunk, she stopped to show them something special: an old newspaper. It was written half in English and half in an unfamiliar language.

"What is this?" asked Jenny.

"That's the ***Cherokee Advocate***," Granny said. "Papa used to read it to us kids. And that's Cherokee **syllabary**. Our written language. Not many people use it now, but at one time we used it to fight for rights as Cherokees."

"Granny, can you speak Cherokee?" asked Becca.

"A few words," replied Granny. "We were supposed to speak English in school so we were never taught our language, but Papa and our grandparents spoke Cherokee."

Ꮣ da Ꮤ ta Ꮥ de Ꮦ te Ꮧ di Ꮨ ti

Ꮬ dla Ꮭ tla Ꮮ tle Ꮯ tli

Ꮳ tsa Ꮴ tse Ꮵ tsi

Ꮹ wa Ꮺ we Ꮻ wi

Ꮿ ya Ᏸ ye Ᏹ yi

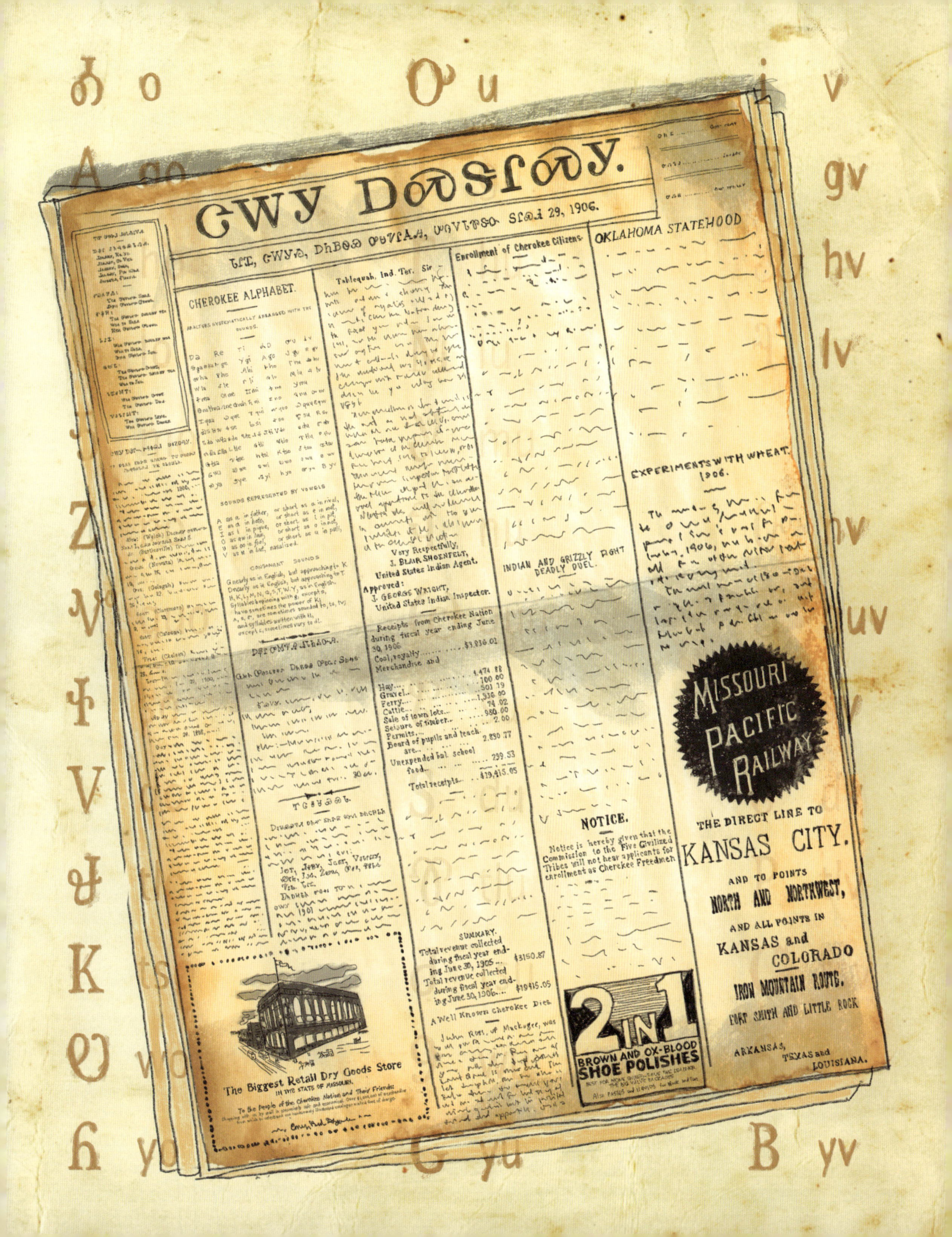

CHEROKEE ALPHABET.
SOUNDS REPRESENTED BY VOWELS
CONSONANT SOUNDS
Tahlequah, Ind. Ter. Sir
Very Respectfully,
J. BLAIR SHOENFELT,
United States Indian Agent.
Approved:
J. GEORGE WRIGHT,
United States Indian Inspector.
Receipts from Cherokee Nation during fiscal year ending June 30, 1906
SUMMARY.
A Well Known Cherokee Dies.
Enrollment of Cherokee Citizens
OKLAHOMA STATEHOOD
EXPERIMENTS WITH WHEAT. 1906.
INDIAN AND GRIZZLY FIGHT DEADLY DUEL.
NOTICE.
Notice is hereby given that the Commission to the Five Civilized Tribes will not hear applicants for enrollment as Cherokee Freedmen
MISSOURI PACIFIC RAILWAY
THE DIRECT LINE TO
KANSAS CITY.
AND TO POINTS
NORTH AND NORTHWEST,
AND ALL POINTS IN
KANSAS and COLORADO
IRON MOUNTAIN ROUTE.
FORT SMITH AND LITTLE ROCK
ARKANSAS, TEXAS and LOUISIANA.
2 IN 1
BROWN AND OX-BLOOD
SHOE POLISHES
The Biggest Retail Dry Goods Store
IN THE STATE OF MISSOURI.
To the People of the Cherokee Nation and Their Friends:

Ruth was discovering that she loved to write as much as she loved to read. She wrote short stories about life on the farm and made up little dramas based on articles she read in the newspaper.

But it was poetry that still captivated her. It felt powerful to combine her sense of purpose, her observations, and her Cherokee values into written verse. Poetry allowed her to say everything she felt.

Ruth would recite her work at the dinner table, at school, and even at their neighbors' houses.

She was not shy and she stood out among other children for other reasons too: Ruth had a health condition that made her neck stiff and her head slightly tilted. Plus, she had an unusually strong and mature voice. It was a bit loud, theatrical, and the way she spoke was matter-of-fact. She commanded attention when she spoke.

The Trail of Tears

In the night they shreik and moan
In the dark the tall pines moan
As they guard the dismal trail.
The Cherokees say it is the groan,
Every shreik and echoed groan
Of their forefathers that fell
With broken hopes and bitter fears
On that weary trail of tears.

Broken hopes and broken hearts
A quivering mass of broken hearts
Were driven over the trail
Stifling back the groan that starts
Smothering the moan that
Full four thousand fell;
But still the Great Spirit his people
As they travel the trail of tears.

From the homes their fathers made
From the graves the tall trees shade
For the sake of greed and gold
The Cherokees were forced to go
To a land they did not know,
And Father Time or wisdom old
Cannot erase, through endless years
The memory of the trail of tears.

As Granny sat back in her chair she opened an old shoebox next, revealing what appeared to be a beaten-up notebook.

"Look here," she said, smiling. "Ruth was a writer her whole life. She wrote poems, articles, books and even speeches."

Granny thumbed gently through the notebook until she found what she was looking for.

"Here it is," she said. "This was everyone's favorite poem, 'The **Trail of Tears**.'"

"What is the Trail of Tears?" Becca asked.

Their great-grandmother paused and thought for a moment. "It's a sad story, girls. A long time ago, Cherokees lived in the beautiful Smoky Mountains around North Carolina, Tennessee, and Georgia. But then our ancestors were forced to leave their homes because of a thing called **colonization**. This poem talks about how we can still feel the pain from that horrible experience today."

"Non-Natives took our homes and land and pushed us out. It's called the Trail of Tears because our ancestors were forced to walk nearly a thousand miles in the winter to a place set aside for us called '**Indian Territory**,'" Granny continued quietly. "Thousands of people, mostly our elders and babies, died. My great grandfather, Jackson Muskrat, was just a little boy when his family made the journey west."

"Ruth wrote about this tragedy a lot. In fact, she's one of the people who named it the Trail of Tears through her poetry."

"Did anyone in our family die?" asked one of the girls.

Granny replied, "No. We are lucky. Our family survived."

When Ruth was ten years old, she learned the Cherokee Nation was in trouble again.

Her father came home, feeling more hopeless than ever before.

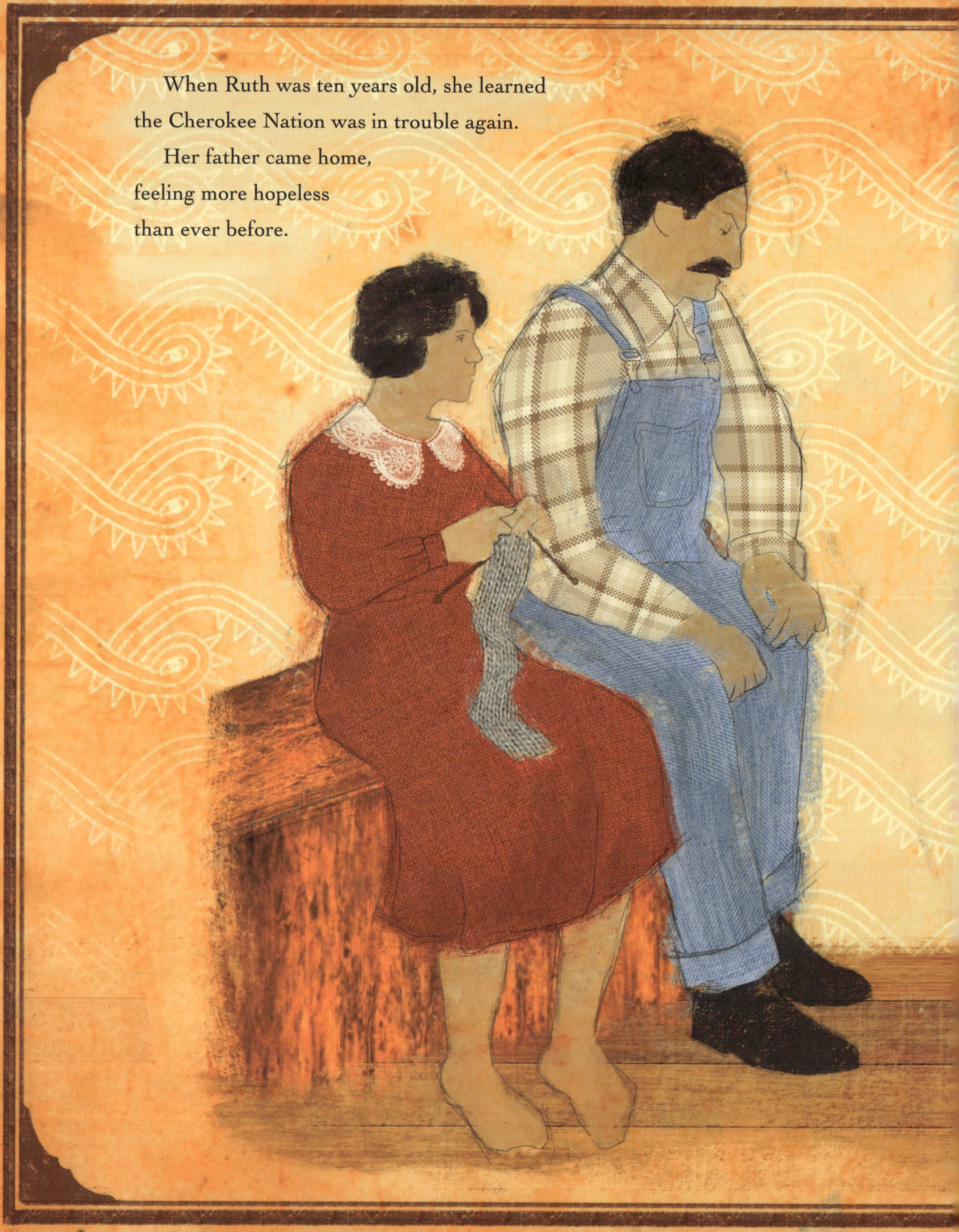

He gathered the family together and told them that the president of the United States was turning their home, Indian Territory, into a new state called Oklahoma.

Despite tribal leaders' best efforts to stop it, the Cherokee Nation was once again in trouble because of the so-called "Indian problem."

Ruth was in disbelief as Papa told them how their community's lands would be divided up and **allotted** to different families, and how some would have to move.

"The Trail of Tears"
by Ruth Muskrat Bronson
Gadugi
The Indian Problem

Ruth thought about losing her beloved Cherokee Nation leaders and her Cherokee neighbors and schools. Without a tribe, she worried Cherokee people would lose their lifeways and the community values that made life so peaceful.

But what troubled her most of all was the sight of her father who seemed completely defeated.

Ruth knew right then it was her time to help.

THE **HEARTACHE** SHE FELT THAT DAY WOULD GUIDE HER THROUGH THE **REST OF HER LIFE**.

Cowskin Prairie Schoolhouse

At just fourteen years old, Ruth left home.
She chased her education, moving from school to school across Oklahoma and later the whole country, never wasting time and never taking no for an answer.

Tonkawa Preparatory School

University of Oklahoma

At each school, she wrote and published her poetry and led student organizations. Everyone knew Ruth was a proud Cherokee from the Cowskin Prairie and that she was determined to change the world.

In 1919, when Ruth was in her early twenties, she took a job with the YWCA, an organization that supported young women. They sent her to the Mescalero Apache **Indian Reservation** in New Mexico.

Similar to home in the Cherokee Nation, there was a strong sense of community on the reservation, but the tribe's leaders had few resources to make life better for their people.

Ruth knew now that there was indeed an "Indian problem" — but it was not the problem Americans were led to believe. The problem was not the Indians themselves. It was how the Indians were treated by **governments** and people. They were not given a voice of their own when important decisions were being made that impacted Native American people.

"Wellll, lookie here!" Granny said excitedly, pulling a newspaper clipping from the box.

"Aunt Ruth went to China?!" one of the girls asked excitedly.

"Yes, and back then it was quite a big deal," said Granny. "She traveled by boat to the other side of the world and spent six months in Peking, China, as part of a cultural exchange, learning about people from other countries and teaching them about Native Americans."

By 1923, Ruth had become a well-known Indian **advocate**. Newspapers all over the United States published articles about her trip to China, her beliefs, and her poetry. At the same time, Native American issues were finally getting the attention of more Americans. People were starting to care.

Ruth and other advocates continuously spoke about the need for change. And then, one day, she learned she was invited to speak at the White House in front of the president of the United States.

"This is it, Papa!" she said excitedly over the phone.

Ruth believed this was her chance to set the record straight, to push for representation, and to help, not only her Cherokee people, but all Native Americans.

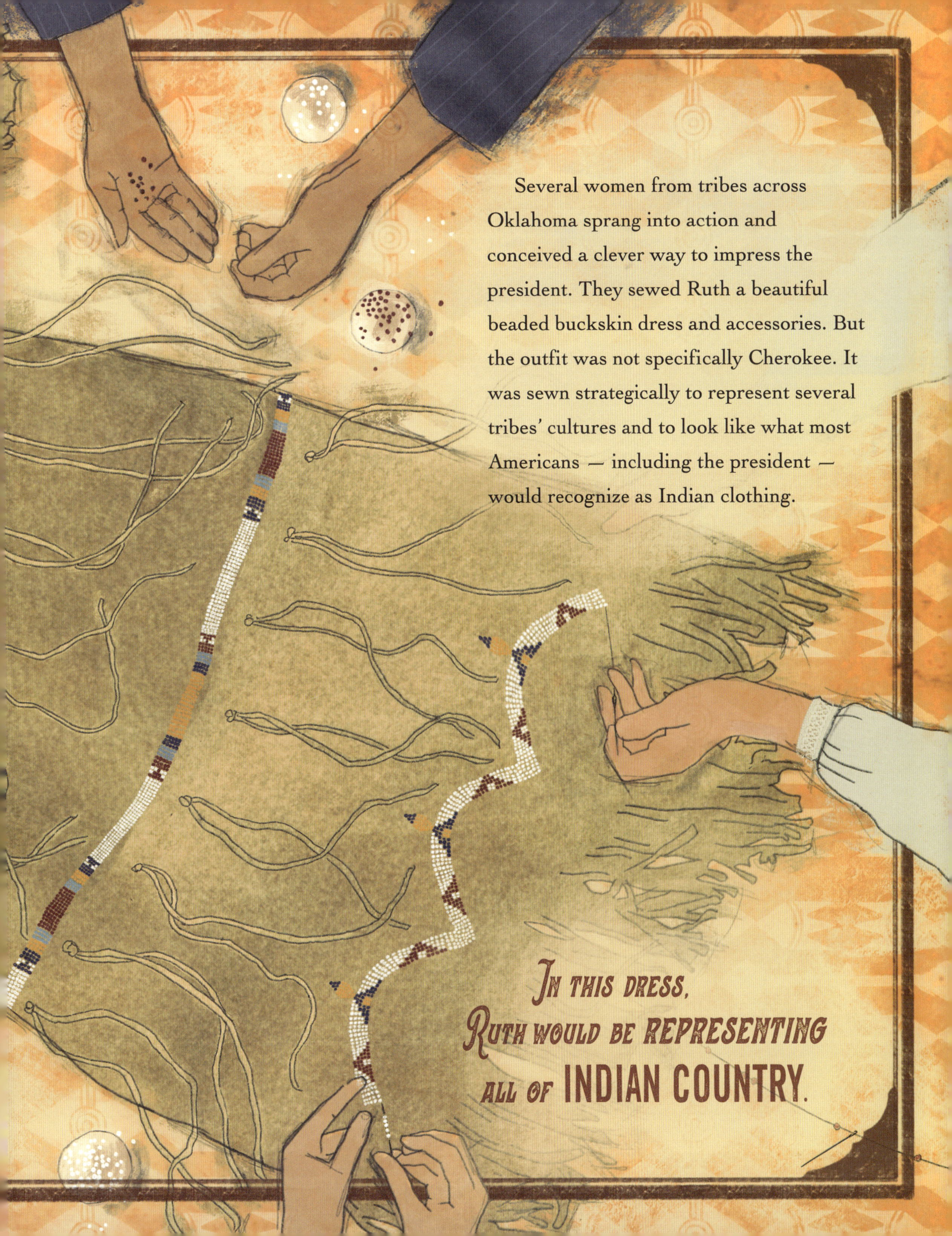

Several women from tribes across Oklahoma sprang into action and conceived a clever way to impress the president. They sewed Ruth a beautiful beaded buckskin dress and accessories. But the outfit was not specifically Cherokee. It was sewn strategically to represent several tribes' cultures and to look like what most Americans — including the president — would recognize as Indian clothing.

IN THIS DRESS,
RUTH WOULD BE REPRESENTING
ALL OF INDIAN COUNTRY.

On December 13, 1923 Ruth gave a speech at the White House, using carefully worded language that appealed to the leaders in attendance while also advocating for Native American youth.

She told **President Calvin Coolidge** that the real "Indian problem" was the hardships imposed upon her people. She boldly stated that the Indian youth of today must be allowed to become leaders — and to guide their people into a new era where they would have a chance to regain their strength as a people and obtain economic independence.

Ruth sternly told the president that Native American people should be allowed to retain their own cultures and community values *and* become citizens of the United States, which would grant them basic civil rights and let them contribute to the building of America.

The girls' jaws dropped, and their eyes widened, as the beaded buckskin dress finally emerged from the trunk . . .

In June of 1924, just six months after Ruth's speech at the White House, President Coolidge signed the **Indian Citizenship Act**. The law granted all American Indians the right to US citizenship.

Ruth believed this was a big step in the right direction for Native Americans. Even though the United States was still mostly run by white men, she had proven that people cared about Native American civil rights, and that they had the power to influence people and policies.

BUT HER **MISSION** WAS NOT OVER . . .

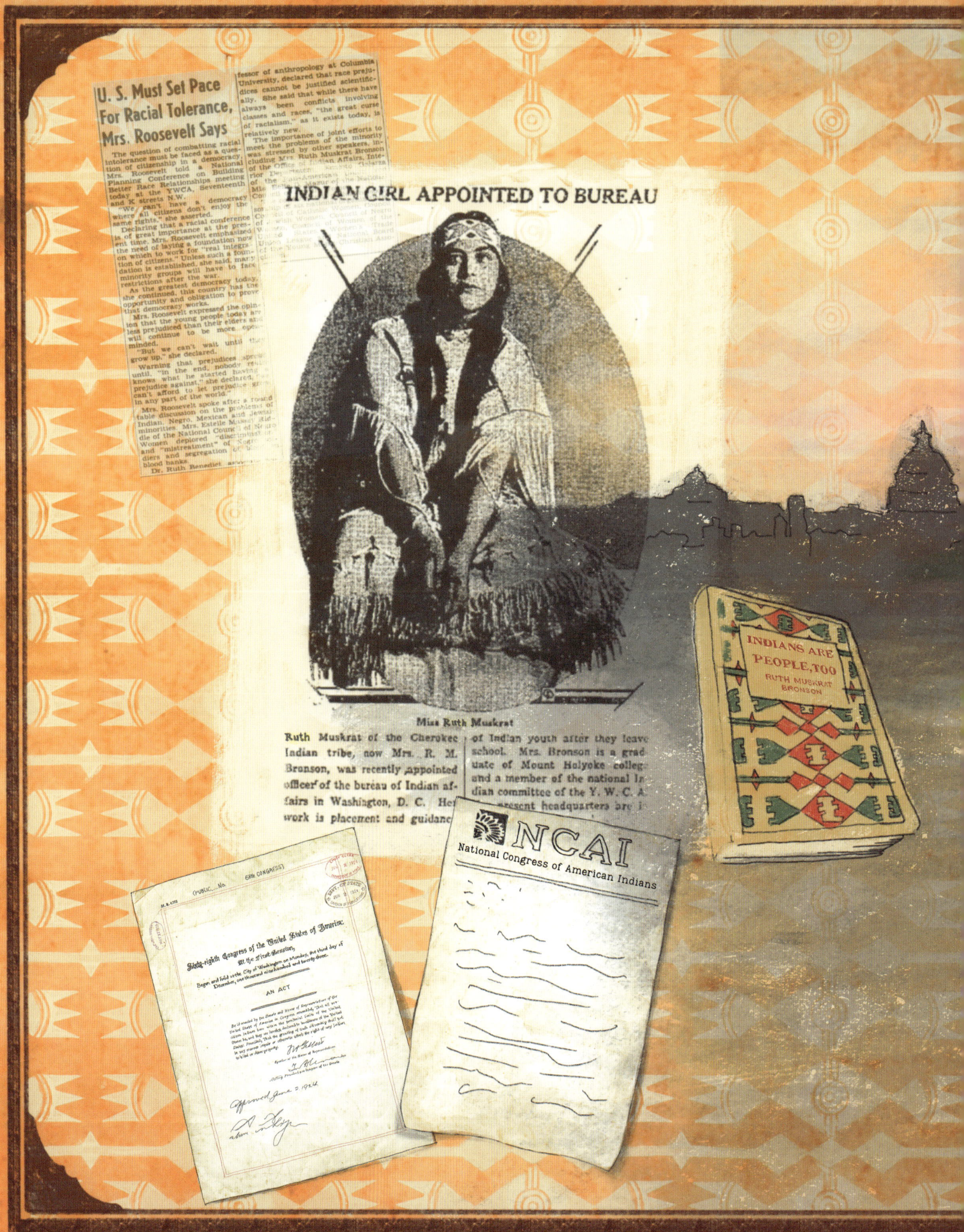
U. S. Must Set Pace For Racial Tolerance, Mrs. Roosevelt Says
The question of combatting racial intolerance must be faced as a question of citizenship in a democracy, Mrs. Roosevelt told a National Planning Conference on Building Better Race Relationships meeting today at the YWCA, Seventeenth and K streets N.W.
"We can't have a democracy where all citizens don't enjoy the same rights," she asserted.
Declaring that a racial conference is of great importance at the present time, Mrs. Roosevelt emphasized the need of laying a foundation now on which to work for "real integration of citizens." Unless such a foundation is established, she said, many minority groups will have to face restrictions after the war.
As the greatest democracy today, she continued, this country has the opportunity and obligation to prove that democracy works.
Mrs. Roosevelt expressed the opinion that the young people today are less prejudiced than their elders and will continue to be more open-minded.
"But we can't wait until they grow up," she declared.
Mrs. Roosevelt spoke after a round table discussion on the problems of Indian, Negro, Mexican and Jewish minorities.
Dr. Ruth Benedict
fessor of anthropology at Columbia University, declared that race prejudices cannot be justified scientifically. She said that while there have always been conflicts involving classes and races, "the great curse of racialism," as it exists today, is relatively new.
The importance of joint efforts to meet the problems of the minority was stressed by other speakers, including Mrs. Ruth Muskrat Bronson of the Office of Indian Affairs, Interior Department
INDIAN GIRL APPOINTED TO BUREAU
Miss Ruth Muskrat
Ruth Muskrat of the Cherokee Indian tribe, now Mrs. R. M. Bronson, was recently appointed officer of the bureau of Indian affairs in Washington, D. C. Her work is placement and guidanc
of Indian youth after they leave school. Mrs. Bronson is a graduate of Mount Holyoke colleg and a member of the national Indian committee of the Y. W. C. A.
INDIANS ARE PEOPLE, TOO
RUTH MUSKRAT BRONSON
Sixty-eighth Congress of the United States of America;
At the First Session,
AN ACT
Approved June 2, 1924
NCAI
National Congress of American Indians

Afterwards, Ruth moved all around the country, holding many jobs working on behalf of Native Americans, until eventually she landed in Washington DC.

In 1928, she married a man named John Bronson. Later, when a friend of Ruth's passed away, they adopted her baby daughter, Dolores, who was from the Laguna Pueblo, a tribe in New Mexico.

While she was busy raising young Dolores, Ruth wrote the book *Indians Are People Too*, which challenged stereotypes and tried to foster a better understanding of Native American people and their lifeways. It was used as a textbook across the country.

In 1944, **the movement** swelled once more. Other like-minded Native Americans began meeting at Ruth's home where they once again practiced gadugi. They ate together, shared stories, and made plans. Ruth became a founder and the first leader of the **National Congress of American Indians**, a powerful political group that still works to make life better for Native Americans today.

Through the years, Ruth continued to work for NCAI, visiting and helping tribes all over the United States including many trips to Alaska and the Southwest. She tried to stop the federal government from taking advantage of tribes and their land through unjust laws and environmental overreach. She was well known to all tribal leaders as she fought to create better lives for their communities.

Despite decades of change-making work, Ruth's heartache never subsided. Native Americans were not granted the full right to vote until 1965, and even then, continued to face more discrimination and unfair governmental policies. The need for vigilance would remain.

Ruth lived out her final years in the Arizona desert, very near the place where she began working to solve the "Indian problem." Even though she was retired, she never stopped helping NCAI or using her influence to push for justice and protection of tribal **sovereignty**.

The Honorable Morris K.
Rayburn House Office Building
Washington, D.C. 20515
Dear Congressman Udall

Under the quiet ticking of her clock, Granny pulled up the covers and wished her great granddaughters a goodnight.

"You girls must always take pride in your Cherokee roots, and you must always tell our stories," she said. "You are all clever and have the power to stand up for what you believe in, just like Ruth."

"Maybe one day we can all get back to living the Cherokee way and take care of one another, the way Papa always wanted. That's what Ruth was fighting for, you know . . ."

That night was cold and still on Granny's farm.

Silence covered the rolling hills of Monkey Island, and the lake shimmered in the peaceful beauty of winter.

The Cherokee Nation was at peace.

Until . . .

DONG!!
DONG!!
DONG!!

Author Note

NEWS · ᏗᏃᏪᎵᏍᎬ

Ruth Muskrat Bronson Day in the CN

In an early photo from 1923, Ruth Muskrat Bronson poses with President Calvin Coolidge and the Committee of 100 on the south lawn of the White House. During her visit, she presented President Coolidge with a copy of Gustavus Elmer Emmanuel Lindquist's book "The Red Man in the United States" and gave a speech on Indian policy, all while wearing regalia that reflected pan-Indian cultural identity.

"By the time Ruth was pressing our case across Indian Country in Washington, D.C., it was a dark time in the history of this country … in which terminating the tribes was the order of the day."

Principal Chief Chuck Hoskin Jr.

ing a bit more of an enlightened approach to its treatment of Native Americans. But it didn't happen by accident, and so when I traveled to Washington, D.C., and thought about the ease with which tribal leaders today can interact with high ranking officials of the government, the United States, I realized that we are standing on the shoulders of Ruth Muskrat."

Great-great niece and Senior Director of Cherokee Film Jennifer Loren said "Aunt Ruth" has always been a shining star to her family, who were in attendance at the ceremony from the

tives were openly discriminated against, Ruth would not have it. She grew up in the Cherokee Nation where she was a respected member of her community. So, she surrounded herself with people who believed in her and in a bigger purpose – respect civil rights and education for our people. Ruth was someone who simply got things done. That runs in our family."

With thanks to the *Cherokee Phoenix*

Growing up in Oklahoma in a family full of strong, loving, empowered Cherokee women, we always revered our Great Aunt Ruth, holding her name and accomplishments in the highest regard. As a journalist and novice poet myself, I have marveled at the complexity and wisdom in Ruth's voice, gifted to us through her writing. I have been completely ignited by her passion for Native American rights, and her bravery is something I try to live up to. To me, Aunt Ruth has always been a rock star.

When I began working as a TV host and documentary filmmaker for the Cherokee Nation, I realized that Aunt Ruth's story and work were not well known . . . not in the Cherokee Nation, Oklahoma, or anywhere. Like so many brilliant women throughout history, her impact had somehow slipped into the shadows.

Bringing Ruth's story into the light has been the honor of my life! I have had the opportunity to read her handwritten letters kept in the Smithsonian archives, to dig through the family's heirlooms, and to have conversations with people who knew her and could recall her visionary leadership. This book wouldn't be possible without the tenacity of my sister, the talented Caldecott Medal-winning illustrator Rebecca Kunz, or without the historical knowledge archived and shared by our mother Janet Gann. Working alongside them has been a dream come true. But what excites me most in bringing Ruth's story to life is the idea that generations of young readers could find hope and inspiration in these pages to be curious, brave, and to stand up for what they believe in.

Ruth Muskrat Bronson and generations of our Cherokee ancestors fought every type of battle imaginable so that we could survive and thrive as Cherokees. And here we are. Stoodis!

Wado (Thank you),

ᏃᏙᏏ Jen Loren

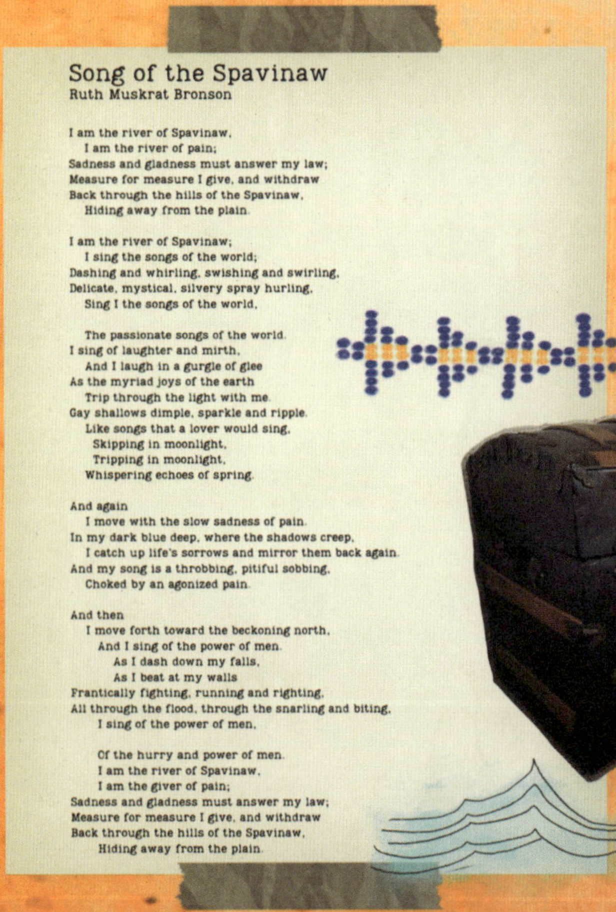
Song of the Spavinaw

Ruth Muskrat Bronson

I am the river of Spavinaw,
I am the river of pain;
Sadness and gladness must answer my law;
Measure for measure I give, and withdraw
Back through the hills of the Spavinaw,
Hiding away from the plain.

I am the river of Spavinaw;
I sing the songs of the world;
Dashing and whirling, swishing and swirling,
Delicate, mystical, silvery spray hurling,
Sing I the songs of the world,

The passionate songs of the world.
I sing of laughter and mirth,
And I laugh in a gurgle of glee
As the myriad joys of the earth
Trip through the light with me.
Gay shallows dimple, sparkle and ripple.
Like songs that a lover would sing,
Skipping in moonlight,
Tripping in moonlight,
Whispering echoes of spring.

And again
I move with the slow sadness of pain.
In my dark blue deep, where the shadows creep,
I catch up life's sorrows and mirror them back again.
And my song is a throbbing, pitiful sobbing,
Choked by an agonized pain.

And then
I move forth toward the beckoning north,
And I sing of the power of men.
As I dash down my falls,
As I beat at my walls
Frantically fighting, running and righting,
All through the flood, through the snarling and biting,
I sing of the power of men,

Of the hurry and power of men.
I am the river of Spavinaw,
I am the giver of pain;
Sadness and gladness must answer my law;
Measure for measure I give, and withdraw
Back through the hills of the Spavinaw,
Hiding away from the plain.

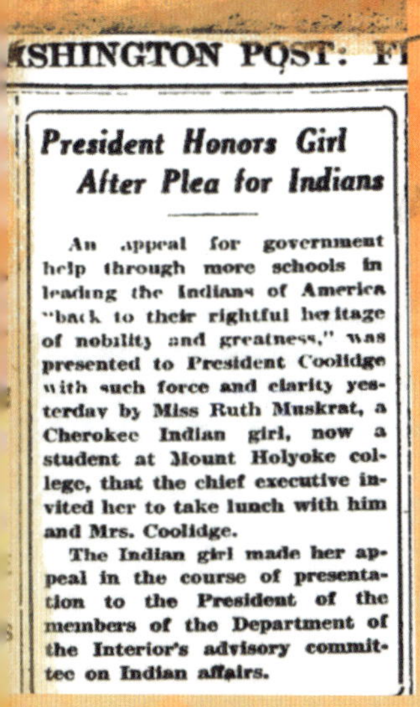
WASHINGTON POST: F

President Honors Girl After Plea for Indians

An appeal for government help through more schools in leading the Indians of America "back to their rightful heritage of nobility and greatness," was presented to President Coolidge with such force and clarity yesterday by Miss Ruth Muskrat, a Cherokee Indian girl, now a student at Mount Holyoke college, that the chief executive invited her to take lunch with him and Mrs. Coolidge.

The Indian girl made her appeal in the course of presentation to the President of the members of the Department of the Interior's advisory committee on Indian affairs.

ILLUSTRATOR NOTE

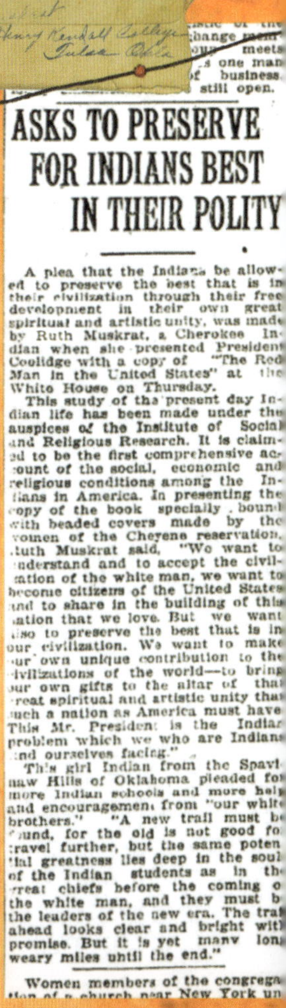
ASKS TO PRESERVE FOR INDIANS BEST IN THEIR POLITY

A plea that the Indians be allowed to preserve the best that is in their civilization through their free development in their own great spiritual and artistic unity, was made by Ruth Muskrat, a Cherokee Indian when she presented President Coolidge with a copy of "The Red Man in the United States" at the White House on Thursday.

This study of tha present day Indian life has been made under the auspices of the Institute of Social and Religious Research. It is claimed to be the first comprehensive account of the social, economic and religious conditions among the Indians in America. In presenting the copy of the book specially bound with beaded covers made by the women of the Cheyene reservation, Ruth Muskrat said, "We want to understand and to accept the civilization of the white man, we want to become citizens of the United States and to share in the building of this nation that we love. But we want also to preserve the best that is in our civilization. We want to make our own unique contribution to the civilizations of the world—to bring our own gifts to the altar of that great spiritual and artistic unity that such a nation as America must have. This Mr. President is the Indian problem which we who are Indians find ourselves facing."

This girl Indian from the Spavinaw Hills of Oklahoma pleaded for more Indian schools and more help and encouragement from "our white brothers." "A new trail must be found, for the old is not good for travel further, but the same potential greatness lies deep in the souls of the Indian students as in the great chiefs before the coming of the white man, and they must be the leaders of the new era. The trail ahead looks clear and bright with promise. But it is yet many long weary miles until the end."

Women members of the congregation of a church near New York un

As children, Jen and I grew up hearing stories of our legendary Aunt Ruth. A woman of grace and incredible strength who could move seamlessly between Indian Country and the Western world. The spirit of Ruth felt both palpable and ephemeral and the imagination of her stories began to live in me. I wanted to know more. Who was this indelible woman who fought so fiercely for Native rights and policies? And why did more people not know about her?

A dream was born . . . the dream of a picture book that would tell her incredible story . . . an accessible biography told through the lens of her descendants. We wanted the world to know this woman.

Ruth came from a lineage of strong women and forged a blazing path for all who came after her. My prayer is that I continue Ruth's legacy and model the same to all children. It has been an honor to tell her story through image. On behalf of Ruth's family, I can only hope that I have celebrated her life legacy honestly and accurately.

Hybrid and traditional Cherokee symbols are woven throughout this story as a visual tool to invoke emotion and meaning. A serpent motif invokes a menacing tone, where uncertainty or despair are present. A generic Native motif from one of Ruth's book covers is reimagined as a traditional wing pattern, an opportunity to reclaim authenticity over stereotypes. A beaded Cherokee star points to the significance of the sacred number seven, which represents the seven directions and the seven clans, among other things. Scissortail Flycatcher, the Oklahoma state bird, flies from page to page, emblematic of Ruth's ability to move between worlds. Additionally, according to Cherokee folklore, when all creatures came to live on Earth, Panther was one of two animals able to stay awake for seven nights. As a result, Panther was gifted with the auspicious power to see at night. Much like Panther, Ruth was stealthy and fierce.

Creating this book with my sister, Jen Loren, has been an absolute passion project. Jen perfectly articulated this story with the beauty and sincerity of Ruth herself. I am forever grateful to our mother, Janet Gann, our family historian, who listened intently to her grandmother's stories. And thank you to the Cherokee Nation, which has not only overcome indelible challenges, but continues to rise above and thrive, despite them.

Wado (Thank you),

Rebecca Lee Kunz

Timeline

October 3, 1897 — Ruth Margaret Muskrat is born on the Cowskin Prairie in Indian Territory (now Delaware County, Oklahoma). Her father was James Ezekial Muskrat (Cherokee) and her mother was Ida Kelly Muskrat (Irish).

1912–1916 — Ruth attends the University Preparatory School and Oklahoma Institute of Technology in Tonkawa, Oklahoma, where she begins publishing poems

and essays about Cherokee life and serving in organizational leadership roles.

1919 — Ruth attends the University of Oklahoma.

1920 — Ruth leads a summer recreation program on the Mescalero Apache Reservation in New Mexico, inspiring her continued advocacy for all Native Americans.

1922 — Ruth travels to the World Conference of Student Christian Volunteers in Peking (Beijing), China, and participates in cultural exchanges.

1923 — Ruth delivers a historic speech at the White House as part of the Committee of 100 on American Indian Affairs, urging fairness and improved education for Native people. She presents a hand-bound book called *The Red Man in the United States* to President

Calvin Coolidge. President Coolidge invites her to return the next day, where she has lunch with the president and First Lady in the Rose Garden.

1925 — Ruth graduates from Mount Holyoke College with a degree in English and a growing reputation as a writer and advocate. She teaches at Haskell Institute in Lawrence, Kansas, before she becomes the first guidance and placement officer for the Bureau of Indian Affairs (BIA), helping Native students continue their education and find meaningful work.

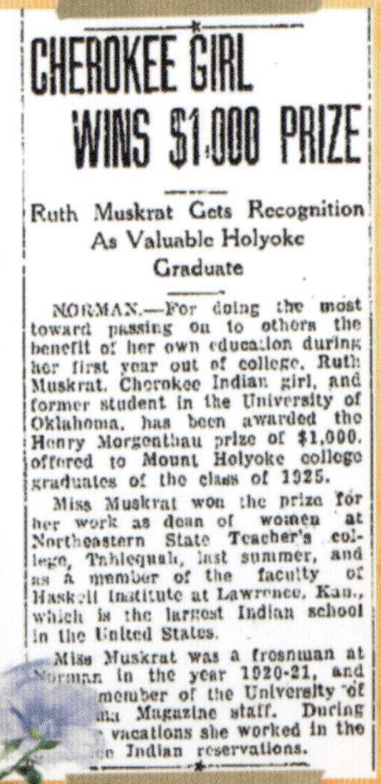

CHEROKEE GIRL WINS $1,000 PRIZE

Ruth Muskrat Gets Recognition As Valuable Holyoke Graduate

NORMAN.—For doing the most toward passing on to others the benefit of her own education during her first year out of college, Ruth Muskrat, Cherokee Indian girl, and former student in the University of Oklahoma, has been awarded the Henry Morgenthau prize of $1,000, offered to Mount Holyoke college graduates of the class of 1925.

Miss Muskrat won the prize for her work as dean of women at Northeastern State Teacher's college, Tahlequah, last summer, and as a member of the faculty of Haskell Institute at Lawrence, Kan., which is the largest Indian school in the United States.

Miss Muskrat was a freshman at Norman in the year 1920-21, and member of the University of Magazine staff. During vacations she worked in the Indian reservations.

1925 — Ruth is hired as the Dean of Women at Northeastern State

Teachers College in Tahlequah, Oklahoma. She writes widely for national publications and gives speeches across the country on Native education, sovereignty, and the importance of preserving Indigenous cultures.

1928 — Ruth marries John Bronson and begins work at the BIA in Kansas City, Missouri, overseeing educational counseling.

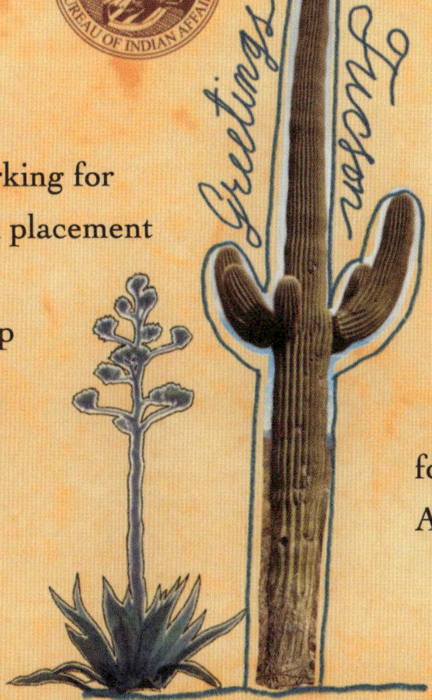

1930 — Ruth begins working for the BIA as a guidance and placement officer in charge of the Federal Indian Scholarship and Loan Program. She also serves as director of the Indian Welfare Committee of the General Federation of Women's Clubs, working to build national support for Native communities.

1935 — Ruth moves to Washington, DC, and directs health and welfare programs for Native families and works as a field representative supporting improved living conditions and tribal self-determination.

1939 — Ruth earns a master's degree in public education from George Washington University. Ruth and John adopt a twenty-one-month-old child, Dolores, from the Laguna Pueblo.

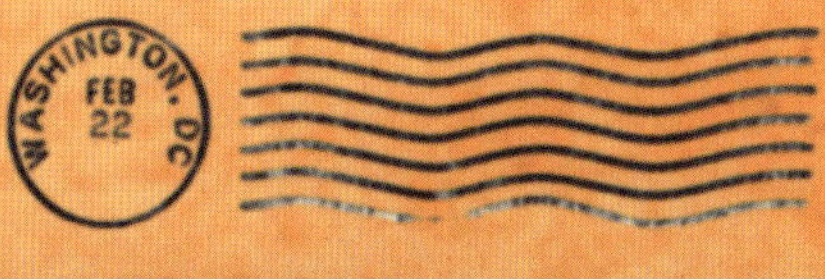

1943 — Ruth resigns from the Bureau of Indian Affairs "to be with family."

1944 — Ruth's book *Indians Are People Too* is published by Friendship Press. Ruth plays an important role in the formation and early years of the National Congress of American Indians (NCAI), serving as its first executive director from 1944 to 1948.

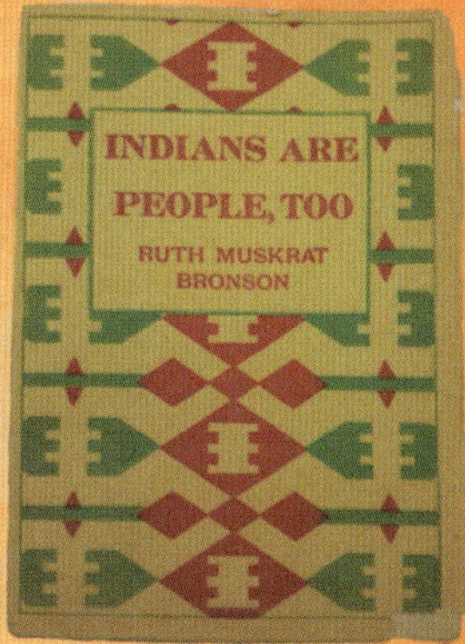

1950s–1960s — Ruth and John move to Arizona, where she begins working for the US Health Service as a health education specialist for the San Carlos Apache Reservation.

1962 — Ruth retires from all government service. She becomes a field representative for the Save the Children Federation in Tucson, Arizona, working closely with the Tohono O'odham and Yaqui peoples.

June 12, 1982 — Ruth Muskrat Bronson passes away, leaving a legacy of courage, education, leadership and unwavering dedication to Native Nations.

Dec. 13, 2023 — Principal Chief Chuck Hiskin Jr declares Ruth Muskrat Bronson Day in the Cherokee Nation.

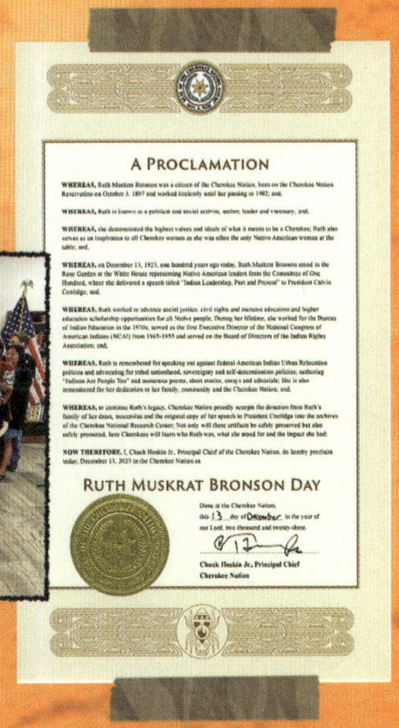

With thanks to the Cherokee Nation

Here's what's cookin' Snow Ice Cream Serves 8
Recipe from the kitchen of Thelma Lee

1 Gallon clean snow
1 Cup sugar
1 tsp vanilla
2 Cups milk

Mix sugar, vanilla, and milk in large bowl. Stir in snow. Serve!

GLOSSARY

Page 5

Snow Ice Cream Recipe — Gather fresh, clean snow in a big bowl. Stir in sugar, a little sweetened condensed milk, and a splash of vanilla. Mix until creamy. Enjoy quickly before it melts!

Blackberry Cobbler Recipe — Mix blackberries with sugar and a bit of flour. Pour into a baking dish. Cover with biscuit dough or cake batter. Bake until golden brown. Delicious with ice cream!

Page 10

Indian Territory — A large area of land where many Native Nations, including the Cherokee, were forced to move in the 1800s. Much of it later became the state of Oklahoma.

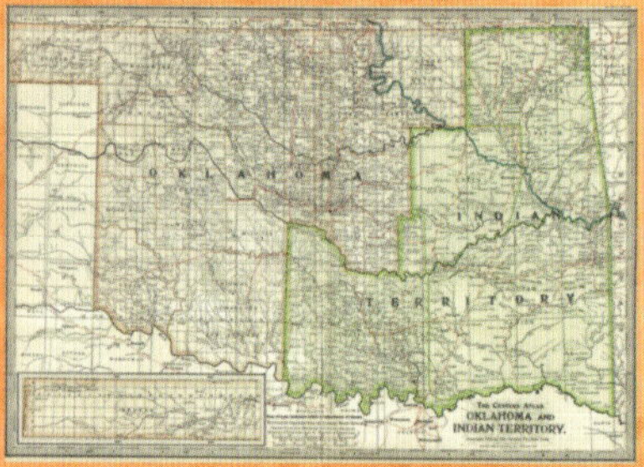

Oklahoma — Oklahoma became the 46th state of the United States on **November 16, 1907**. Before that, it was made up of Indian Territory and Oklahoma Territory.

Page 15

Gadugi (SSY) — A Cherokee word that means *working together for the good of the community*. It is an important Cherokee value.

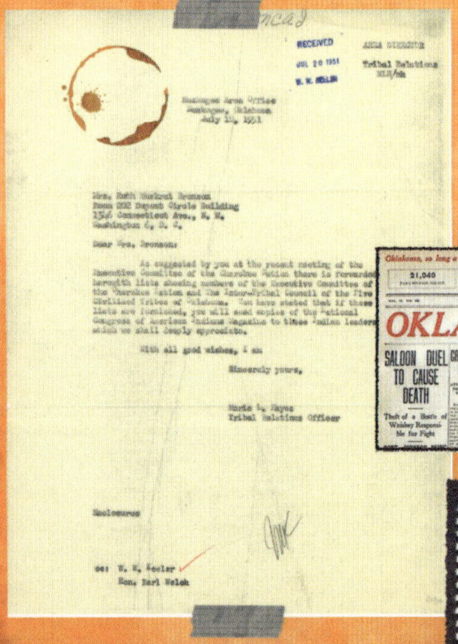

Oklahoma, so long a maverick of the southwest, has finally received the coveted brand of statehood and been admitted to the corral

THE DAILY OKLAHOMAN

OKLAHOMA BECOMES STATE

SALOON DUEL TO CAUSE DEATH

Theft of a Bottle of Whiskey Responsible for Fight

CROOKEDNESS IN BROOKLYN BANKS

FIREBUGS STILL TERRORIZE ENID

HOUSE ROBBED IN BROAD DAYLIGHT

SCRATCH OF QUILL PEN LETS THE NEW STATE INTO UNION

"That Makes Oklahoma a State," Says Roosevelt, When He Affixes Signature

INDIAN TERRITORY AND OKLAHOMA ARE SYMBOLICALLY WED

Thirty Thousand People Attend the Inaugural Ceremonies at State Capital

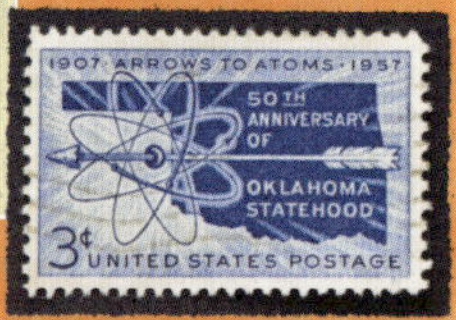

Page 19

Integrity — Doing the right thing, even when no one is watching.

Page 20

Keetoowah Society — A Cherokee traditional group that worked to keep Cherokee culture, language and ceremonies alive, especially during hard times. (Pictured left before a stomp dance, ca. 1917.)

With thanks to the Oklahoma Historical Society

Page 21

Indian vs. Native American — The word *Indian* was first used by explorers who thought they had reached India. For many years, the US government used the word *Indian*. Today, many people prefer *Native American* or the names of their own Nations (like Cherokee), because they are more accurate and respectful. Some Native people still use *Indian* to describe themselves and it's still used as a legal term in the US government.

"The Indian Problem" — A phrase US leaders used in the 1800s and early 1900s when they wanted Native peoples to give up their land, culture, and languages. It appeared in government reports and policies that pushed for assimilation.

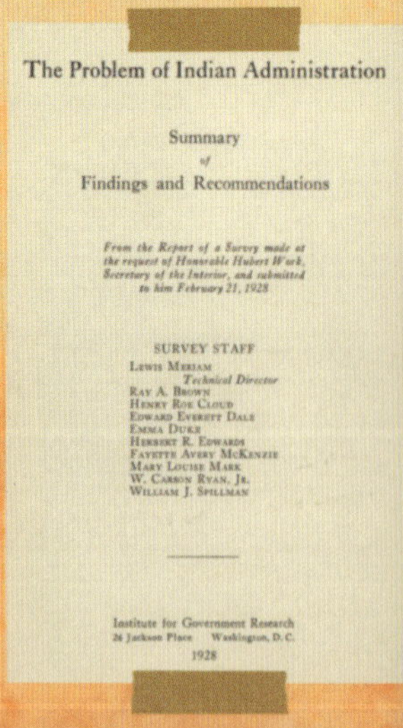
The Problem of Indian Administration

Summary
of
Findings and Recommendations

From the Report of a Survey made at the request of Honorable Hubert Work, Secretary of the Interior, and submitted to him February 21, 1928

SURVEY STAFF
Lewis Meriam
Technical Director
Ray A. Brown
Henry Roe Cloud
Edward Everett Dale
Emma Duke
Herbert R. Edwards
Fayette Avery McKenzie
Mary Louise Mark
W. Carson Ryan, Jr.
William J. Spillman

Institute for Government Research
26 Jackson Place Washington, D.C.
1928

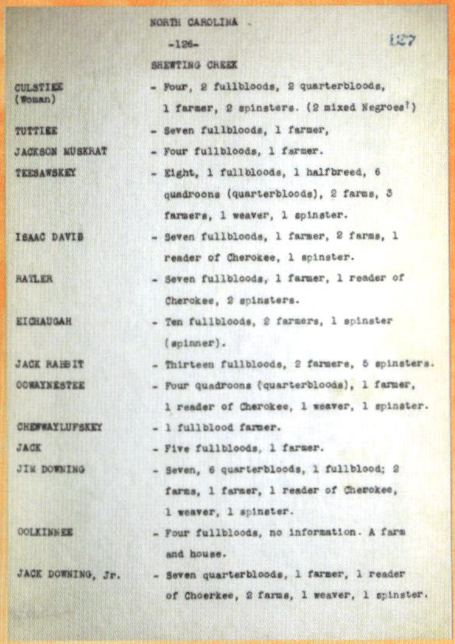

NORTH CAROLINA

-126- 127

SHEWTING CREEK

CULSTIEE (Woman)	- Four, 2 fullbloods, 2 quarterbloods, 1 farmer, 2 spinsters. (2 mixed Negroes?)
TUTTIEE	- Seven fullbloods, 1 farmer,
JACKSON MUSKRAT	- Four fullbloods, 1 farmer.
TEESAWSKEY	- Eight, 1 fullbloods, 1 halfbreed, 6 quadroons (quarterbloods), 2 farms, 3 farmers, 1 weaver, 1 spinster.
ISAAC DAVIS	- Seven fullbloods, 1 farmer, 2 farms, 1 reader of Cherokee, 1 spinster.
RATLER	- Seven fullbloods, 1 farmer, 1 reader of Cherokee, 2 spinsters.
EICHAUGAH	- Ten fullbloods, 2 farmers, 1 spinster (spinner).
JACK RABBIT	- Thirteen fullbloods, 2 farmers, 5 spinsters.
OOWAYNESTEE	- Four quadroons (quarterbloods), 1 farmer, 1 reader of Cherokee, 1 weaver, 1 spinster.
CHEWWAYLUFSKEY	- 1 fullblood farmer.
JACK	- Five fullbloods, 1 farmer.
JIM DOWNING	- Seven, 6 quarterbloods, 1 fullblood; 2 farms, 1 farmer, 1 reader of Cherokee, 1 weaver, 1 spinster.
OOLKINNEE	- Four fullbloods, no information. A farm and house.
JACK DOWNING, Jr.	- Seven quarterbloods, 1 farmer, 1 reader of Choerkee, 2 farms, 1 weaver, 1 spinster.

Assimilate — To make one smaller culture become like another larger culture. US policies tried to make Native people stop speaking their languages and living in their traditions and instead act like white settlers.

Page 23

Ancestors — Family members from long ago. Ancestors are very important in Cherokee culture and traditions.

Page 34

The Cherokee Advocate — A newspaper written in both the Cherokee language and in English that began in 1844. It shared news and helped keep the Cherokee language strong. Cherokees had another newspaper called *The Cherokee Phoenix* that began printing in 1828 and was the first newspaper published by a tribe.

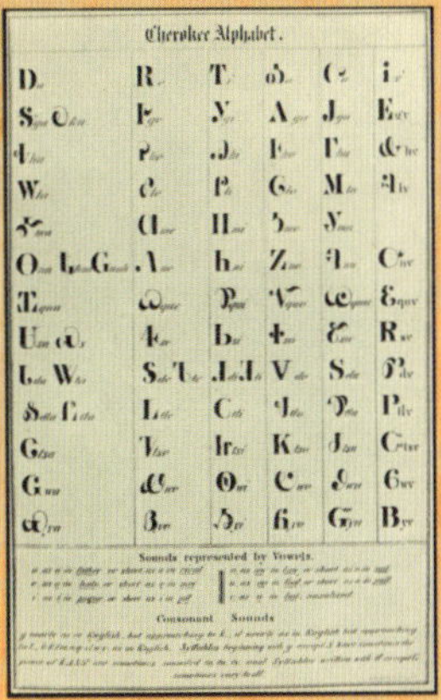

Syllabary — A special writing system invented by Sequoyah so the Cherokee language could be written down. Each symbol stands for a syllable (like *ga* or *li*).

Page 39

Trail of Tears — The thousand-mile journey (outlined in the map right) Cherokee and other Native Nations were forced to take when they were removed from their homelands in the southeastern United States. Thousands suffered and died along the way. From the Cherokee view, it was a time of deep loss, but also of survival. According to the Smithsonian Institute, Cherokee writer and educator Ruth Muskrat Bronson was among the first Native Americans who used the name "Trail of Tears" to describe the forced removal.

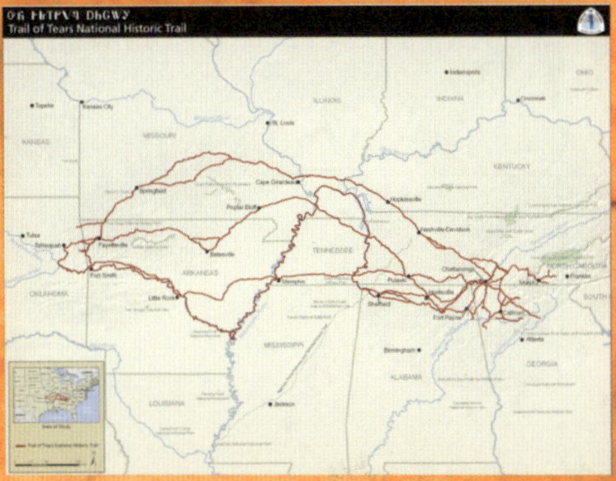

With thanks to the Trail of Tears Association

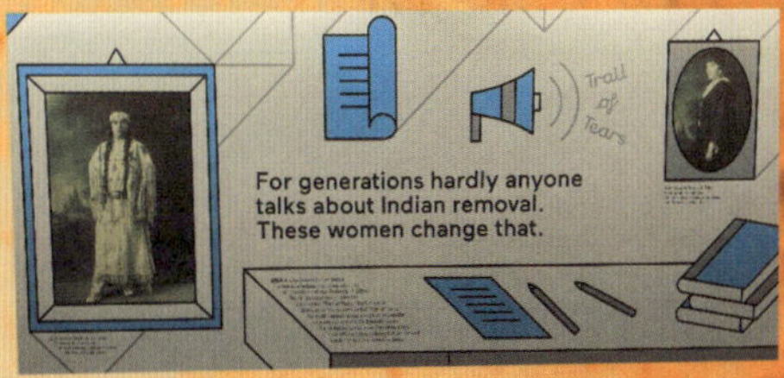

With thanks to the National Museum of the American Indian / Smithsonian

Colonization — When people move to a land where others already live and take control of it, often making the original people (like Native Americans) lose their homes, land, and way of life.

Page 43

Allotted Land — Land given to individual Cherokee families instead of being held by the Nation. This was part of US policies that broke up tribal lands. When communally-held Cherokee land was "allotted" that means it was split into small pieces for each family to own, which made it much easier for other people to buy, take, or trick them out of their land.

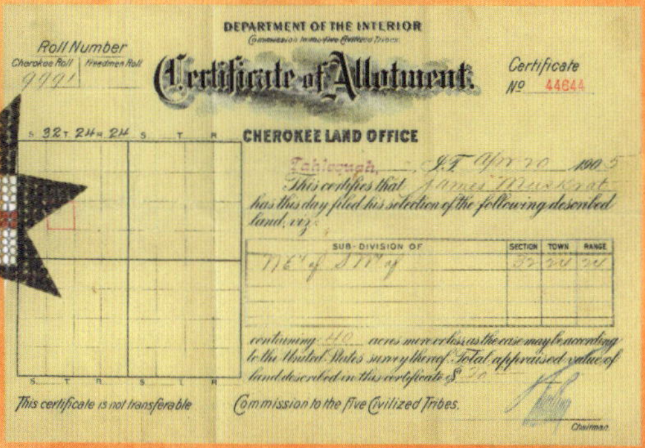

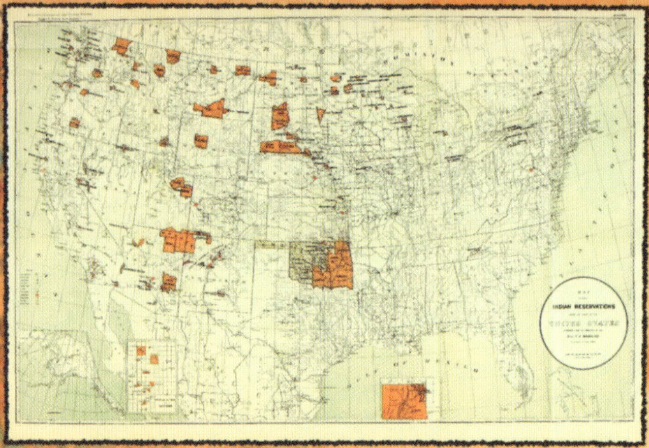

Page 48

Indian Reservation — Lands set aside for Native Nations to live on, often in treaties with the US government. Many were created after tribes were forced off their homelands.

Page 49

Federal Government — The national government of the United States. In the 1920s, it created policies like boarding schools and land allotments as part of its "Indian Problem" approach.

With thanks to the Vine Deloria Papers, Yale Collection of Western Americana, Beinecke Rare Book and Manuscript Library

Page 52

Advocate — A person who speaks up and fights for the rights of others. Ruth Muskrat Bronson was a Native rights advocate. Other well-known Native advocates include Zitkála-Šá, Charles Eastman, and Vine Deloria Jr (pictured left).

Page 57

President Calvin Coolidge — US president from 1923–1929. He signed the Indian Citizenship Act in 1924.

Coolidge was known for being quiet and serious, earning him the nickname "Silent Cal." His presidency is remembered for a time of economic growth called the "Roaring Twenties," but also for not doing much to stop unfair treatment of Native Americans and other communities.

Native Americans and Citizenship — In the early 1900s, most Native Americans were not considered US citizens, even though they were born in the United States. This meant they couldn't vote or have equal rights.

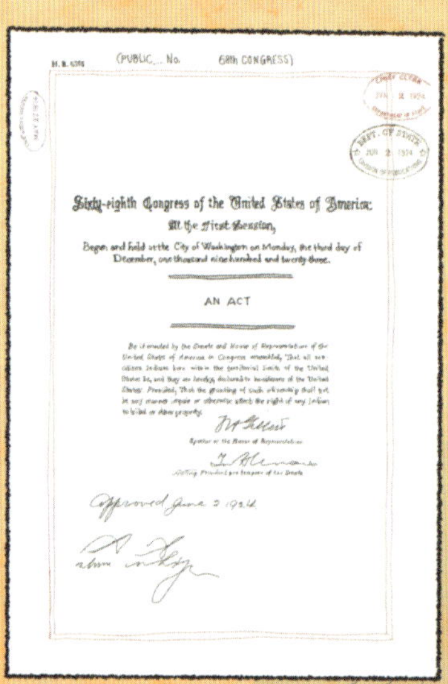

(PUBLIC, No. 68th CONGRESS)

Sixty-eighth Congress of the United States of America;
At the First Session,
Begun and held at the City of Washington on Monday, the third day of December, one thousand nine hundred and twenty-three.

AN ACT

Be it enacted by the Senate and House of Representatives of the United States of America in Congress assembled, That all non-citizen Indians born within the territorial limits of the United States be, and they are hereby, declared to be citizens of the United States: Provided, That the granting of such citizenship shall not in any manner impair or otherwise affect the right of any Indian to tribal or other property.

Speaker of the House of Representatives

Acting President pro tempore of the Senate

Approved June 2, 1924.

Page 60

Indian Citizenship Act (1924) — A law that gave US citizenship to all Native Americans. While many Native Americans celebrated this change, some tribes opposed it because they believed it was imposed without their consent and threatened tribal sovereignty and traditional governance. Many Native Americans also felt that citizenship could be used to force assimilation and did not guarantee the full rights of US citizens. For example, several states continued to deny Natives voting rights for years afterward.

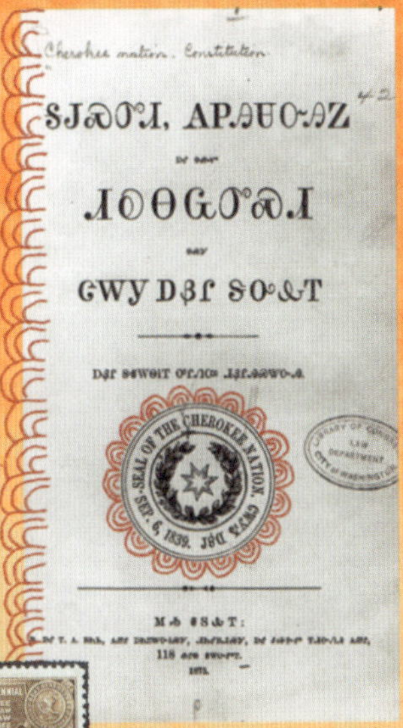

Pages 64-67

"The Movement" — The long fight by Native people for justice, respect, and rights. It includes many movements, such as protecting Native lands, preserving Native languages, fighting for civil rights, and honoring treaties. Important movements include AIM (the American Indian Movement, founded in 1968), the fight against termination policies in the 1950s, the Red Power movement of the 1960s and 70s, and modern movements like Standing Rock (NoDAPL) to protect water and sacred land.

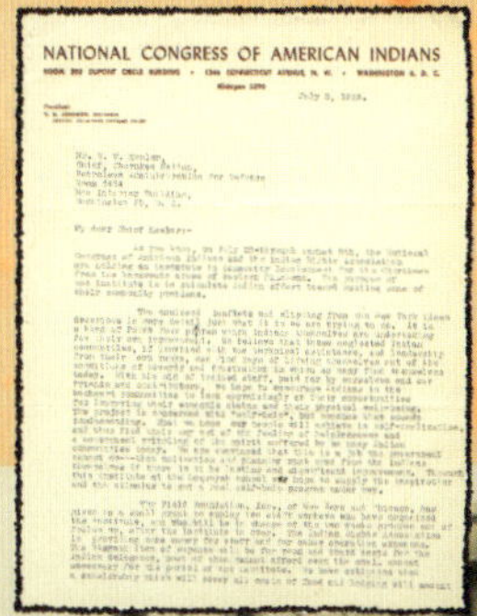

Pages 65

NCAI (National Congress of American Indians) — Founded in 1944, this group works to protect Native rights and support Native Nations. (Pictured below at its charter convention in 1944.)

Pages 68

Sovereignty — Sovereignty means that Native American tribes have the right to govern themselves. They can make their own rules, choose their leaders, and protect their culture and traditions.

National Anthropological Archives, Smithsonian Institution, NAA.PhotoLot.75-33

Study Guide

Themes

✦ Identity & Culture — Ruth fights to preserve Cherokee lifeways and civil rights.
✦ Education & Empowerment — She believes knowledge protects Native communities.
✦ Courage & Advocacy — Ruth boldly speaks truth to power and helps organize movements.
✦ Family & Community — Cherokee Gadugi emphasizes working together and helping one another.

Questions

1. Where and when was Ruth Muskrat Bronson born?
2. How did Ruth feel about reading and learning as a child?
3. What is the meaning of the Cherokee word *Gadugi*?
4. Why were Cherokee families in Indian Territory worried about the US government's actions?
5. What inspired Ruth to begin writing poetry?
6. How did Ruth show leadership while she was still in school?
7. What political event led Ruth's father to be sad?
8. Why did Ruth travel to the Mescalero Apache Reservation?
9. What made Ruth realize there was a different "Indian problem" than the one Americans talked about?
10. What country did Ruth travel to as part of her advocacy work?
11. What messages did Ruth share with President Calvin Coolidge?
12. What law was passed shortly after Ruth's White House speech?
13. What did the Indian Citizenship Act do?
14. How did Ruth continue helping Native Americans after her speech?
15. What organization did Ruth help establish?
16. What was the name of the book Ruth authored?
17. How did Ruth's parents influence her values and determination?
18. What major historical event involving the Cherokee Nation did Ruth often write about?
19. If Cherokee people never became part of greater American society (whether through forced assimilation or choice), how do you think that would have affected them? What do you think that would that look like in today's society?
20. Why is Ruth Muskrat Bronson remembered as a hero today?

Activities

✦ Write a poem about your family or culture.
✦ Research a Native American leader and write a one paragraph summary of their legacy.
✦ Map the Trail of Tears.
✦ Write a short story about a time when you were brave.
✦ Research the proposed state of Sequoyah and learn which US President denied its establishment and why.
✦ Brainstorm ways your class can practice Gadugi.

SOURCES LIST

Sources

Bronson, Ruth Muskrat. *Indians Are People Too*. Friendship Press, 1944.

Bronson, Ruth Muskrat. *Shall We Repeat Indian History in Alaska?* 1947.

Harvey, Gretchen G. *Cherokee and American: Ruth Muskrat Bronson, 1897–1982*. Ph.D. dissertation, Arizona State University, 1996.

Brown, Kirby. *American National Biography*. "Bronson, Ruth Muskrat." 2020.

The Encyclopedia of Oklahoma History and Culture. "Bronson, Ruth Margaret Muskrat."

Academy of American Poets. "Ruth Muskrat Bronson."

Mount Holyoke College Archives, Alumnae Records.

Bronson, Ruth Muskrat, National Congress of American Indians records; National Museum of the American Indian Archive Center, Smithsonian Institution.

Cherokee Nation Research Center. "Ruth Muskrat Bronson Materials." Accessed 2026.

Personal family archives of Jen Loren and Rebecca Lee Kunz

Additional Historical Sources

Debo, Angie. *And Still the Waters Run: The Betrayal of the Five Civilized Tribes*. Princeton University Press, 1940.

Prucha, Francis Paul. *The Great Father: The United States Government and the American Indians*. University of Nebraska Press, 1984.

Deloria, Vine, Jr. *Custer Died for Your Sins: An Indian Manifesto*. University of Oklahoma Press, 1969.

Smithsonian National Museum of the American Indian. Treaty with the Cherokee, 1835 (Treaty of New Echota), Dec. 29, 1835.

United States Congress. The Dawes Act (General Allotment Act), 1887.

United States Congress. The Curtis Act of 1898.

Perdue, Theda. *Cherokee Women: Gender and Culture Change, 1700–1835*. University of Nebraska Press, 1998.

Mihesuah, Devon A. *American Indigenous Women: Decolonization, Empowerment, Activism*. University of Nebraska Press, 2003.

ADDITIONAL RESOURCES

Ruth Muskrat Bronson, a short documentary by Jen Loren
QR CODE (shown on right): https://osiyo.tv/ruth-muskrat-bronson/

Cherokee Language learning materials:
https://language.cherokee.org/learning-materials/
https://language.cherokee.org/media/tmre3lgz/syllabarychart.pdf
https://language.cherokee.org/media/h1zhnrpb/phonetics.pdf

Indian removals to Oklahoma timeline:
https://www.okhistory.org/research/removal

White House Historical Association article about Ruth Muskrat:
https://archives.whitehousehistory.org/fotoweb/archives/5017-Digital-Archives/Main%20Index/Presidents/Calvin%20Coolidge/1132477.tiff.info

Cherokee Phoenix article about Ruth Muskrat Bronson Day in the Cherokee Nation:
https://www.cherokeephoenix.org/news/dec-13-is-declared-ruth-muskrat-bronson-day-in-the-cn/article_4f5e9398-a009-11ee-923a-d3c3f5a13ff9.html

From the White House Historical Association: "The December 1923 Native American visit to the White House and Ruth Muskrat's speech may have influenced Coolidge to support and sign the 1924 Indian Citizenship Act on June 2." Read more here: Calvin Coolidge and Native Americans – White House Historical Association (whitehousehistory.org)

Library of Congress archived photo of:
Committee of 100 on Indian Affaires – b&w film copy neg. | Library of Congress (loc.gov)

The Mount Holyoke archived photo of the beaded book cover Ruth presented to President Coolidge at the event and the text of her speech, Ruth Muskrat's Speech to President Coolidge, December 13, 1923 – Alumnae Association (mtholyoke.edu)

Mount Holyoke article and additional photo: Mount Holyoke Alumna Embraced Both Parts of Her Cultural Identity – Alumnae Association (mtholyoke.edu)

Oklahoma Historical Society article: Bronson, Ruth Margaret Muskrat | The Encyclopedia of Oklahoma History and Culture (okhistory.org)

Find-A-Grave site:
https://www.findagrave.com/memorial/48165845/ruth-bronson

This book is dedicated to our Great Aunt Ruth.
Your legacy lives on in these pages, and in all who learn from
your strength, courage and stories. We will continue to ring the bell!
—Jen & Becca

This is an Arthur A. Levine book
Published by Levine Querido

LQ
LEVINE QUERIDO

www.levinequerido.com • info@levinequerido.com

Levine Querido is distributed by Chronicle Books, LLC

Library of Congress Control Number: 2026936824
ISBN 978-1-64614-699-4

Printed and bound in China

MIX
Paper | Supporting responsible forestry
FSC
www.fsc.org
FSC™ C008047

Published in October 2026
First Printing

The text was set in Cochin and the title type was hand-lettered.
Book design by Patrick Collins

The mixed media illustrations
were done by Rebecca Lee Kunz featuring a blend
of digital collage, painting, and drawing.